LIFE IN LONDON

by Luckner Pierre

blog: www.londonversusparis.wordpress.com

Life in London
in cinemas December 2020

Cover design by Natacha Lacosse at www.Lcreativeconcept.acossi.com

Published by Amazon on 12/12/18

Breath of Courage
in music stores July 2019

*Dedicated to the heart and soul of London
through the breath of love*

"Where there is hope there is life,
where there is life there is possibility,
and where there is possibility change can occur."
- Jesse Jackson

"We make a living by what we get, but we make a life by what we give."

- Winston Churchill

CONTENTS

Acknowledgements

Thanks to Almighty God for giving me spiritual wisdom and a heart of encouragement to live for His glory and to encourage the heart of humanity. Thanks to Amazon. Thanks to Annette Thornalley for providing six weeks of free accommodation. Thanks to Maria Lenn of Suited and Booted for allowing me to volunteer on a regular basis. Thanks to Wichet for giving me short-term employment and thanks to Aek. Thanks to Tracey Hamilton for the free computer classes.

Thanks to Pret A Manger, Crisis Skylight, Holy Cross Centre Trust, Westminister Kingsway College, Recovery College. Thanks to Christine Redford for choosing my friendly personality for the role of Father Christmas in 2017 and 2018. Thanks to Ben for sharing Ghanian food with me. Thanks to the North London Church of Christ and to Christ Church Fulham. Thanks to all the volunteers and coordinators in the Friday Mission Lunch ministry. Thanks to Sensi Armando for his generosity to my teenage life. Thanks to Tammy Mesdaieu and to my aunts for their generosity. Thanks to Francis Ansong for his generosity to my future in London. Thanks to Herve for his generosity and for our friendship. Thanks to Parkview Cafe for all the lovely breakfasts. Thanks to the Poetry Library in London.

Thanks to every reader for taking the time to read this book that will guide the human conscious through the breath of love.

With Thanks,
Mr. Luckner Pierre

Introduction

Because this book is about my life in London, I prefer to use British English in writing this book.

When I arrived in London in late summer 2016, I had to live in a backpacker hostel for four weeks until I could find stable accommodation.

While living in the hostel, I created an account on the Spareroom website and on the Christian Flatshare website in order to help me find a single room in Greater London.

However, if I had more money for accommodation at that time, I would have slept at a hotel where I would have my own room.

Before I found a single room two months later through one of my classmates at my college, the hostel was the only way to avoid homelessness.

In regard to hostels, the team of managers at every hostel should separate the male adults from the female adults to protect the privacy of people and to consider how this reliable solution will be a positive outcome for the future.

In the basement of the hostel, I met a Cameroonian woman who came to London for long-term employment and to learn English.

At the time, I had to speak basic French with her because she was not immerse in the English language.

She told me that her CDD contract in France kept being renewed because her French employer refused to give her a CDI contract, which is unlawful and surprising.

On the day of her appointment in central London for a national insurance number, we went to the JobCentre Plus. At the desk, I kindly translated from English to French to help her complete her application form.

When we returned to the hostel, I then referred her to Training Link so she could take the ESOL course to help her improve her English.

Although many French people live in London for employment or educational studies, they still need to speak basic English in order to communicate their wants and needs.

On the other hand, formerly important for its airport in 1915 to 1959, Croydon has gained recognition in Greater London and still this London Borough is remembered in the hearts of many Londoners and visitors.

While still living in a hostel in September 2016, I saw the cheapest price for a single room to let in Croydon on the Spareroom website. When I arrived in front of the house, I waited almost twenty minutes for the landlord.

When the landlord arrived, he and I walked upstairs to the single room.

When he opened the room door, I did not see a bed in the room, and the room is about ten square metres.

Indeed, the landlord should have considered buying a small bed for the room to alleviate the financial burden upon future tenants.

In addition, this bedless room did not have a closet nor a drawer to store clothes.

This landlord must have had selfish intentions. Without a car in London,

it would cost me money to hire a van to bring the bed into the room if I wanted to buy a small bed. On one hand, it was funny to see a room without a bed. On the other hand, it was very disrespectful to the sensitivity of tenants.

Overall, the landlord should have been generous to provide a small bed for the room for the comfortability of accommodation to tenants. I am glad I did not rent this bedless room.

Though London has become my favourite city due to the rich history of diversity and the good manners of Londoners, I also have my dislikes about this great city.

For example, I dislike the high cost of living and the severe delays in the mornings at tube stations. For example, while minimum wage still remains under £8 per hour, the cost of public transportation and the cost of accommodation continue to increase on an annual basis. In addition, in regard to buying a house in Greater London, if I wanted to buy a house in Greater London (zone 4), the average cost for a house in North London is £500,000.

The market value of houses in Greater London is extremely expensive and overwhelming.

On the other hand, until this day, I am still cultivating the British way of thinking. Indeed, in the future, I will have a British mentality yet not a British accent because it is almost impossible for my adult life to have a British accent. The British accent makes my heart dance like a professional dancer on stage. I have yet to meet the British version of Pierre. If the British version of Pierre exists in Great Britain, I believe a meaningful friendship will quickly develop through faith and serve a meaningful purpose. I would be ecstatic.

On the other hand, after writing and self-publishing my first book about Paris and how the dark forces of the French environment affected my wellbeing in the past, I decided to write this book and compete against myself in a friendly fashion just to see which book would win the friendly battle. I hope my book about London wins the friendly battle against my book about Paris. GO LONDON! GO LONDON! GO LONDON!

London is one of the cities where English-speaking writers have a valuable opportunity to reach more people from around the world and engage in a multicultural environment.

My hope is I want people to value the rich history of diversity in London and not only focus on the high cost of living.

While the size of Great Britain remains small compared to the United States, the Americans living in the UK continues to contribute their taxes and labour of love to the British economy.

Indeed, I truly believe London is the most diverse city in the world because more than three hundred languages are spoken in this city and there are no majority. In early autumn 2016, I visited Westminster Kingsway College and I met the media production instructor near the front entrance.

When I told the instructor about my educational background in accounting and my interest in video production, he urged me to join the level 3 media production course. At that time, neither the college nor the instructor encouraged me to take an assessment for evaluation. Before anyone is allowed to take a level 3 course at a college, an assessment is usually the first step to determine academic strengths and weaknesses.

During the course of attending classes every week, I learnt essay-writing is required every week and there would be no multiple-choice exam, which discouraged my confidence.

As the debt of tuition kept swimming in my mind, I applied for a student loan only to find out I do not qualify for the loan because at the time I had lived in the United Kingdom for less than three years.

After two months, I withdrew from the media production course and focus on long-term employment.

In my London journey, this learning experience taught me even college instructors can be led to faulty logic if wise precautions are not taken and that human intelligence needs to be guided by the intuition of wisdom.

London is refreshingly beautiful from the inside out. I love the heart and soul of London. GO LONDON! GO LONDON! GO LONDON!

Chapter 1

Her Generosity Shines

"Servants of generosity are unseen amongst us."
- Mr. Pierre

After living for four weeks in a backpacker hostel in central London, one of my Parisian church friends kindly referred me to one of her British friends who helped me find short-term accommodation while I was still searching for long-term accommodation.

When I visited this white British woman for the first time,

I shared my Paris journey and my poetry book, and she shared her Paris experience as she was making coffee in the kitchen. After drinking some coffee in the living room, she gave me the door key and allowed me to live in one of the rooms in her flat for six weeks.

Although my church friend and this British woman are close friends and are cat lovers, I tried to draw the connection between us because before anyone allows a person to live in his or her flat or home there needs to be a familiar bridge between two people.

However, this white British woman was very generous with her flat and kind-hearted. It all came unexpected yet I appreciated this favour of support.

As the days and weeks progressed, I shared my college essay that was for my UCAS application. She provided intuitive feedback that penetrated my soul and stimulated my critical thinking skills.

We did not have much in common, yet we were both cat lovers who love the presence of cats. When I told her that I would write a book about her beautiful cat, she laughed and displayed a joyful smile, yet it was hypothetical and relevant to my love for cats.

While I was still on my bed one morning, her cat jumped on the bed and I guess this cat wanted my attention. I gently touched her cat and her cat was happy to see a new face in the flat.

Before I left her flat to live in another London borough, I gave her a trophy of appreciation and a letter of gratitude because I never met a person who allowed me to live in her flat without a familiar bridge between two people.

Until this day, this unforgettable experience rests deep in my heart as a symbol of God's Grace. Her generosity still shines in my conscious. I love her generosity.

Chapter 2

Employment through Grace

"We make a living by what we get, but we make a life by what we give."

- **Winston Churchill**

After I successfully completed the Food Safety course as my short-term goal to stabilise myself in the British economy, I was qualified to work in a Thai restaurant.

When I used to work in the Thai restaurant, the group of Thai employees treated me like family at the very beginning.

Two months later, the manager hired a new Thai waitress to work two or three days per week.

Before the Thai restaurant opened, I would clean the exterior door panel and the windows next to the panels with a clean sponge and window-cleaning spray.

On the weekdays when the British waitress was working,

one of the Thai waitresses, British waitress and I would eat dinner together and talk about Thai food.

At that point, I began to love Thai food, and it became one of my favourite foods.

On the days when the British waitress was not working,

the Thai waitresses never ate at the same table where the employees ate dinner. It did not bother me, yet it was still peculiar to the sense of teamwork.

One evening when I brought the tray of Thai food upstairs to the new waitress, who was responsible for serving the food to customers, she gave me the impression that I should speak Thai with her.

Though I quickly learnt a few expressions of the Thai language, the Thai waitresses should have been considerate and patient.

For example, if I was working with non-Haitian employees in a Haitian restaurant, I would never show favouritism and I would never force people to speak Haitian Creole because Haitian Creole is not a requirement in an English-speaking country.

When I joined the North London Church of Christ and told my manager about my commitments to this church,

they were very unhappy about the change of my work schedule although they approved the two days of rest.

Few weeks later, the supervisor released me from employment, and I felt that if my manager and supervisor do not respect the commitments of my Christian faith, then I need to find another job in a different industry.

As the old saying goes: "When one door closes, another door opens by the Grace of God."

Because the catering industry is very demanding, I firmly decided to withdraw from this industry.

Overall, I greatly appreciate this short-term employment as it paid for the hours I worked and paid service charges added to my monthly salary in order for me to pay my rent.

With my last salary at this Thai restaurant, I was able to pay two month's rent. When I went to collect my last pay slip, I gave my manager my 4-page testimony and a letter of appreciation.

I thank God and I am grateful to God for opening a new door of employment and positioning me in the right place to share my testimony with people for Him. To God be the glory.

Chapter 3

Generous in London

"Irrepressible generosity flows like a river."
- Mr. Pierre

In November 2016, while I was studying Food Safety for my short-term goal, the Optician Department of Crisis Skylight, a charity organisation, generously gave me free prescription eyeglasses.

At that time, I really needed a pair of eyeglasses, and my heart was grateful and joyful because a new pair of eyeglasses would have costed me at least £200.

In December 2016, my job coach referred me to Suited and Booted, a charity organisation that generously gives dress suits to people who desperately need a dress suit for a job interview.

When I arrived in the room of dress suits, an Irish woman, who was one of the volunteers, could not find my size.

After about ten minutes, she found one dress suit that fit my body frame. When I tried the large suit, I knew it was the right one, and the colour of the suit gave me a positive impression. Suited and Booted gave me a dress suit.

On the other hand, while working at the Thai restaurant to finance my accommodation in London, Crisis Skylight financed the cost of transportation on my Oyster card for five weeks.

I felt a sense of relief because the cost of transportation in London is very overwhelming and all Londoners share this financial burden.

In January 2017, I registered for the free photography course at Crisis Skylight and learnt the three pillars of photography.

In January 2019, after I gave my grant application to my job coach, Crisis Skylight generously financed the cost of the D80 camera, tripod and editing software for my photography-film studies.

Throughout every week, I reflect on the generosity of Crisis Skylight and Suited and Booted, and my humble goal is to be an instrument of generosity in every aspect of helping humanity for God who deserves every second of my life. The gratitude of Grace leads to the generosity of selfless love. Generous giving refreshes my heart and soul and makes me feel alive again.

Chapter 4

Volunteering is a Lifestyle

> "To be really happy and really safe,
> one ought to have at least two or three hobbies,
> and they must all be real ."
> - Winston Churchill

At the Recovery College in Camden, a group of people including myself auditioned as volunteers in a play that reflected the recovery journey for people who have social issues in life through an empathetic approach.

When it was time for me to audition in front of the playwright and two female organisers in the small room, they heard my American accent and they wanted me to play the narrator alone, and I felt very confident about this role because the presence of the mentor-mentee relationship in the monologue grabbed my attention because the practice of one-on-one mentorship appeals to my core values.

As the days and weeks progressed, I received email reminders to see which day all of us could rehearse together in a relaxing environment.

On certain evenings in my bedroom, I read the monologue to myself and memorised the first and last paragraph because I struggled with the two paragraphs in the middle although I have a sharp long-term memory.

On one Sunday afternoon, we rehearsed and each of us became aware of time management for each scene.

The woman, who wrote this play, encouraged me to skip some lines of the monologue to help me articulate the major details for time management purposes.

On the day when we had to perform on a small stage in front of at least twenty-five people, one of the volunteers felt irritated by the adjustment given by one of the female organisers, and this irritation rubbed off on other volunteers.

However, I encouraged this volunteer to remain calm and to maintain her composure because actors and actresses must always stay in character to ensure their performance is effective to the audience.

After our performance, the audience clapped and displayed joyful smiles and there was a sense of appreciation and a positive impact on the audience that led to fellowship and mutual enjoyment.

This volunteer experience was productive, proficient and practical as it reflected the recovery journey for people with social issues. It was refreshingly invigorating and enjoyable in all aspects of the play. Thanks to the Recovery College for the email invitation to audition and thanks to the playwright and two female organisers for the acting support.

Chapter 5

Manmade Opinion Creates Chaos

**"Based on biblical evidence throughout every generation,
God's opinion is more practical than man's opinion in all areas of life."**
- Mr. Pierre

When I met one of the church leaders of the North London Church of Christ (part of ICOC) near Liverpool street tube station, I shared my living testimony to help him have a clear picture of my difficult upbringing in Miami. At that time, I was unaware of his intention to keep me away from other Bible-based churches. On a weekly basis, this church leader and I met for some coffee to discuss the meaning of restoration and this brought encouragement to my life. At one of our weekly meetings, he encouraged me to attend Friday's midweek service at his church because the concept of discipleship teaches Christians to be engaged in the lives of other Christians as this is what Jesus taught his disciples in his ministry. At the same time, whenever he would send text messages and emails to me, the church leader would add a third party in the messages without me knowing although I maintained my faithfulness through faith. On Sunday evenings, I attended another church where Christians focus more on the gift of prayer and prophecy through the supernatural power of the Holy Spirit. Because this particular Bible-based church offered gospel-related courses, I felt more connected to this church than to the North London Church of Christ. After three months of meeting and visiting his church on Fridays and Sundays, he showed me a biblical scripture in the book of 2nd John and then he tried to convince me that I should not visit other churches who are not part of the ICOC because he believes other churches do not have the same biblical curriculum, which is fallacious and judgemental.

Here is the scripture:

2 John 1 :10-11 says, "If anyone comes to you and does not bring this teaching, do not take them into your house or welcome them. Anyone who welcomes them shares in their wicked work (NIV)."

When he showed me this particular scripture to support his opinion, it gave me a strange impression because his way of reasoning generalised other churches and he wanted to satisfy his opinion. Underneath the surface, it was clear that his intention was not straightforward in regards to his view of other churches. Faulty and eccentric. On the contrary, if this church leader had applied this biblical scripture to the right context, such as immoral people in the world, then his reasoning would make perfect sense without being judgemental. The right context supported by biblical scriptures would make perfect sense by faith. Although this church leader had spiritual wisdom, he forgot to recognise that one of the goals of the Christian faith is to be unified with other believers of other churches as this is what Jesus did with those who were not part of his ministry and that the holy presence of the Holy Spirit lives in every church. The problem is some church leaders opinionate the Holy Bible to satisfy their intentions and this fallacy will continue to cause divisions in the field of Christianity. Not to discourage anyone, in my intellectual journey, I have met more closed-minded Christians than open-minded Christians and this could create a spiritual imbalance in any church if precaution is not taken.

Overall, if an opinion does not fit in the equation of biblical truth, it remains chaotic and can easily mislead any generation. Every Christian should have the intention of faith to visit other churches because the body of Christ is made up of different people who have different backgrounds and different testimonies. Manmade opinion creates chaos while Godmade opinion through the Christian faith creates meaningful friendships in Christ.

Chapter 6

Servant or Slave

"A servant's mentality transforms the inner nature of the human heart."
- Mr. Pierre

In different social environments, one will find snobbish intellectuals and friendly intellectuals. Depending on the character traits of people and the evolving circumstances, people are either a servant to humanity or a slave to pleasing other people for self-satisfaction.

In the field of general intelligence, there are different types of intelligence: spiritual intelligence, emotional intelligence, social intelligence, artificial intelligence, philosophical intelligence and many more.

However, if two personalities are intellectually compatible yet are not spiritually compatible this creates friction and a stubborn resistance that produces a negative reaction on the potential friendship that could develop through integrity and mutual understanding.

In all types of intelligence, the nature of each intelligence must always be guided by spiritual wisdom that supersedes and purifies the human flesh.

For example, when I became a follower of Christ, I gained spiritual intelligence through faith that guided me in my academic studies, which led to academic success and graduation. However, if I did not have spiritual intelligence developed in my inner heart, chances are I would not have succeeded at my college because my strengths depend on the activation of spiritual intelligence and my weaknesses were superseded by vitamins and minerals of spiritual wisdom like antibacterial protection.

For more than seventeen years, I have been a servant of spiritual intelligence that connect me to other intellectuals in different environments.

Although it is natural for intellectuals to have disagreements in regards to different subjects because every personality is different, all intellectuals must have a heartfelt understanding of the significant difference between the resistance of selfish pride that leads to self-sufficiency and the mechanism of teamwork about life as a journey or else one's journey will meet painful disappointments.

The power of intelligence can take one's journey to new heights and to different levels of path exploring intellectual diversity.

The interaction of truth through any form of intelligence will determine the prophecy of one's future. Faulty intelligence leads to faulty logic that results in a cycle of human mistakes.

Never be a slave to the skeleton of human intelligence yet grow one's intelligence to be a servant of spiritual wisdom that prevails and never fail in one's journey to everlasting life.

Chapter 7
Poetry Library in London

> "Nourish your hopes, but do not overlook realities."
> - Winston Churchill

After I submitted my poems in different poetry competitions, the campus librarian told me about the Poetry Library in London.

After writing a fascinating essay about London in February 2018, my essay won the writing competition at my college campus and I was proud of myself. I then received a laminated certificate and a book token. I truly believe this was a sign of literary growth in my writing career. I highly valued this literary experience in my courageous heart. Thanks to my college for promoting this literary contest.

On 18th January 2018, I visited the poetry library for the first time and became an active member.

While still there, I learnt this poetry library has the most comprehensive and accessible collection of poetry from 1912 in Britain, and it maintains the concept of modern poetry.

If I did not live in London and meet the campus librarian, I probably would not know about the poetry library in London.

I truly believe to know more about intellectual activities in any city one must live and absorb the ingredients of the city for at least one year as residential living increases the awareness of ongoing activities as it should benefit the poetry community.

Chapter 8

Father Christmas in Enfield

"Success consists of going from failure to failure without loss of enthusiasm."
- Winston Churchill

After I applied for the role of Father Christmas on the indeed website, the store manager quickly contacted me and we exchanged emails to confirm the interview date.

When I introduced myself to the manager, she needed to ask me some questions to see if I was the right person for this Christmas job.

Later on that day, the manager called me and told me that I qualify for the job based on my reliability and confidence.

Before I began working this job in November 2017, I forgot to do research on the character of Father Christmas that could have improved every interaction with children in the grotto, an artificial cave for Santa Claus.

As the Christmas day approached, I wrote a Christmas poem "Christmas Loves Children."

I even thought about writing a Christmas poetry book as a gift to children who visited me in the grotto, yet I saved this realistic idea for the future.

Although the story of Father Christmas and his reindeers is imaginary and hypothetical, I still had to act as Father Christmas and preserve the Christmas spirit in the conscious of these children, which was fun and joyful.

On a few occasions, the manager told me that there were some parents who liked my interaction with their children while others were not pleased.

With the help of my manager's advice and research on the Wikipedia website,

I became more aware of potential choice of words that would encouraged children to smile and fully enjoy their time in the grotto.

On one Saturday morning, when my manager came to give me my pay slip in the grotto, I gave her a trophy of appreciation as a Christmas gift because this Christmas job became my favourite job in my London journey.

Though the monthly salary was an average of £300 per month, this Christmas job made me feel connected to the Christmas spirit in the heart of London, and I appreciated every aspect of this role like irrepressible generosity. Even when I find better employment opportunities in the future, this Christmas job will forever live in my conscious and breathe in my soul like the waves over the sea.

I am glad I gained volunteer experience as Father Christmas for two years in the Friday Mission Lunch where I volunteer as it positioned me in the direction of the British-American connection in London. Ho, Ho, Ho, Happy Christmas.

Chapter 9
Open-Mic Night in Hackney

"Don't cry because of what you lost,
Smile because of what you learned."

- Personal Motto

In January 2018, I visited an open-mic night in Hackney for the first time. After I wrote my name on the list to perform my poem, I met the male organiser and his personality was very friendly.

Although not many people attended this event, the few who came that night enjoyed my poem 'Life of a Volunteer' and 'Racism Pollutes the World.'

Afterwards, I enjoyed others perform and there was a sense of positive energy that flowed like an electric guitar. Before I left this venue, one person purchased my poetry pamphlet for £2. Though I am not a famous poet, I felt the feeling of appreciation because someone supported my poetry pamphlet.

At that time, I did not self-publish the paperback format of my poetry book because there is still a low demand for poetry books in the market and this reminded me that most people will not buy my poetry book.

Ten months later, I self-published the paperback format on the Amazon website. I still do not expect people to buy my poetry book, yet if I continue engaging the audience in open-mic events it may encourage even a small audience to purchase the e-book or paperback format at any time.

If any bookstore in the world needed me to promote my poetry book for international poetry day, I would travel anywhere in the world even if it just sold one copy because I believe this valuable experience will create a fan base for the future.

Chapter 10

Poetry Performance at the British Museum

"Courage is what it takes to stand up and speak. Courage is also what it takes to sit down and listen."

- Winston Churchill

Two weeks before the first of July, the arts manager of Crisis Skylight sent me an email invitation asking me to perform two poems in three minutes on the overall theme of evolution at the British Museum.

When we arrived at the front entrance of the British Museum, someone gave us name tags and led us to the area where champagne, sparkling water and refreshments were served. After interacting with new people and drinking plenty of water to stay hydrated, we returned to the front entrance to meet the man who would introduce the poets including myself on stage. While we waited and stared at the JTI Choir performance who were on stage, we enjoyed shredded barbecue chicken, pita chicken wrap and some chocolate and strawberry ice cream in a small cup. Then, it was time for us to perform our poetry pieces on stage in front of at least one hundred people in attendance. When I shared my two poems, I felt confidently anxiety-free and so did the other two poets. After the three poets including myself performed our poetry piece, the audience clapped and displayed joyful smiles. Then, I gave my poetry pamphlet to at least three individuals who expressed their appreciation of my poetry performance. My hope for future poetry performances is to promote a poetry album as a fundraising activity for Crisis

Skylight, even if it reaches only a small audience, and to find literary sponsorships that should enable me to have leisure time for poetry-writing. Although my poetry book will never sell a hundred copies in the publishing industry and I still have not won a poetry competition due to poetry being subjective, I am still proud of myself and of the other two poets who shared their poems at the museum. This wonderful experience built a good reputation for Crisis Skylight as it showed a strong engagement in the entertainment value of poetry. If I had the paperback format of my poetry book, this could have generated word of mouth in future interactions.

Thanks to Crisis Skylight for the invitation and thanks to all the guests.

BIO:

Mr. Luckner Pierre is a French-born Haitian-American poet, rapper and screenwriter who highly values his heartfelt poems, hip hop songs and screenplays that speak to the human heart. While still a baby in French Guyana, his father abandoned him and forced his mother to move to Miami, Florida where he experienced physical abuse and racism.

Pierre is a graduate of Miami Central Senior High and Miami Dade College.

His favourite secular rapper is Tupac Shakur and his favourite non-secular rapper is Lecrae.

His favourite Tupac song is *"Mamma's Just A little Girl"* as this song encourages all men to appreciate the value of motherhood and that without women in this world no man would be born.

His favourite Lecrae song is *"I Did It for You"* as this song resonates in his heart as a powerful symbol of hope to alleviate global poverty.

His favourite poet is Pablo Neruda, who won the Nobel Prize for Literature in 1971.

In May 2018, Pierre self-published his inspirational book *"Volunteering is a Lifestyle: More Valuable than Money,"* as it relates to his five years of volunteer experience in Europe.

In March 2018, he self-published his poetry book, *"Courageous Life through Poetry."* Out of all the books he has written,

"Volunteering is a Lifestyle: More Valuable than Money" is his favourite book because he gained more volunteer experience than work experience in Europe and the life as a volunteer gives him joy and the feeling of appreciation.

In May 2018, Pierre wrote a short film about life in Paris where he learned the French language.

In June 2019, Pierre intends to create this film in the heart of Paris, and it will help the world understand the significance of the French language in Europe.

In June 2019, his second book about Paris "Life in Paris" becomes a friendly competition to his first and only book about London "Life in London."

At the age of fifteen, Pierre's first job was cleaning the floor at a local supermarket. Because the labour laws in America do not permit teenagers to work, his manager kept him for only one week, yet Pierre appreciated the job because his father was not there to support him and his mother passed away when he was twelve years old.

His favourite teenage experience was when he took his half-sister to the day care center in the mornings and brought her home in the afternoons after school while his single-parent mother was a bus driver working in the mornings and afternoons.

Pierre believes if he was raised in New York he would have gained acceptance in the New York society as opposed to the Miami society because New York has a reputation of diversity.

While London is still his favourite city, his favourite American city is New York because since the age of thirteen he cultivated the New York state of mind, and he fell in love with the lyrical content of famous New York rappers: *2Pac, Nas, Mobb Deep* and *Notorious B.I.G.*

In fact, his style of rapping is very similar to the typical New York rapper.

Though he loves the British accent with a passion, he will always cherish the New York lifestyle in his courageous heart. On the other hand, Pierre also loves country music as it appeals to his senses and he sees the vision of combining rap lyrics with a country instrumental beat on his first album.

Furthermore, he wants the American country music to integrate with the British country music so there could be a union between the two.

In June 2019, his first studio album *'Breath of Love'* is a reflection of the significance of unconditional love to humanity.

The first single 'Ready to Roll' became a classic single and reaches platinum status and receives international recognition.

His second single 'London to Me' proves to be appreciative and sentimental about his London experience.

In 2019, Pierre wants to promote diversity through multiculturalism and an anti-racism movement to combat against racism in the present and future generations.

In August 2019, his second studio album *'Street Wisdom'* encourages hoodlums to be reconciled with other hoodlums and this album becomes the new standard for the hip hop community.

His forthcoming book *'Street Wisdom'* complements the album and raise awareness of unity in every community and the film version focuses on the theme of brotherly love.

In January 2020, Pierre will self-publish his book ***"Black Power Every Hour."*** In June 2020, Pierre will self-publish his first political book, ***Through Her Intuition: 2020***, to encourage American politics to elect a woman president in October 2020. Pierre is vulnerable yet courageous. Pierre loves Europe with a passion.

About the Author

Pierre earned an Associate in Arts degree from Miami Dade College.

His insightful thinking helped him awaken his senses and develop his spiritual intelligence to write literary books about his real-life experiences with realistic concepts to encourage and enlighten everyone in the world.

His intelligence and integrity has placed him in leadership roles where he can lead people to mentorship, academic success, community involvement and encourage people to break free from irrational cultural beliefs and love humanity. He is interested in anthropology, sociology, philanthropy and charitable activities.

In 2021, Pierre intends to earn a degree in film studies. His humble goal is to become a philanthropist and a motivational speaker. He is determined and destined to set a high standard of excellence in the music and film industry.

His books will continue to impress, inspire, and motivate others for generations to come.

36235339R00022

Printed in Poland
by Amazon Fulfillment
Poland Sp. z o.o., Wrocław